Courageous Candles

A Hanukkah story

Courageous Candles

A Hanukkah story

Joelle M. Reizes and Rabbi Joseph B. Meszler

Illustrated by Kris Graves

PROSPECTIVE PRESS

Winston-Salem

PROSPECTIVE PRESS LLC

1959 Peace Haven Rd #246, Winston-Salem, NC 27106

www.prospectivepress.com

Published in the United States of America by Prospective Press LLC

 TRADEMARK

COURAGEOUS CANDLES
A HANUKKAH STORY

Cover and interior art by Kris Graves
© Prospective Press, 2021

ISBN 978-1-63516-006-2

ProP-G017

Printed in the United States of America
First Prospective Press hardcover printing, November, 2021

The text of this book is typeset in Rum Raisin

Dedicated to our children

Zachary, Eliana, Naomi, Samantha, and Justin

It was almost **Hanukkah**,

and a box of candles sat on a windowsill next to the **menorah**.

The menorah had spaces for eight candles and one extra candle, the helper candle, called the **shamash**.

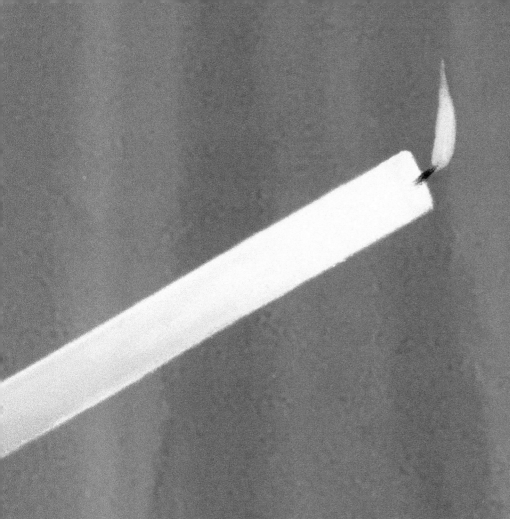

The shamash had a big job. It had to light all the other candles.

Hanukkah
Candles

The candles in the box didn't know if they could be the shamash because it was such a big, important job.

On the first day of Hanukkah, the candle chosen to be the shamash only had to light one candle. It stood tall, lit the candle, and proud it had done its job, melted away in *happiness*.

On the second day of Hanukkah, the shamash had to light two candles. "Easy!" the chosen candle thought. It stood tall, lit the two candles, and proud it had done its job, melted away in *joy*.

On the third day, the candle picked to be the shamash worried

that it couldn't light the candles because three seemed like a lot,

but the other candles said, "You can do it!" It stood tall, lit the

three candles, and proud it had done its job,

melted away in *gladness*.

On the fourth day, the selected candle was very nervous but the other candles said, "You can do it!" So, it took a big breath, stood tall, and lit the four candles. Proud it had done its job, it melted away in *contentment*.

On the fifth day, the candle that was picked worried a lot about

being the shamash, but the other candles said, "You can do it!" It

straightened its shoulders, took a big breath, stood tall,

and lit the five candles. Proud it had done its job,

it melted away in *triumph*.

On the sixth day, the selected shamash turned to its friends and said, "I can't do this. It is too hard." The other candles said, "Yes, you can do it!" It took a big, big breath, stood tall, and lit the six candles. Proud it had done its job, it melted away in *thankfulness*.

On the seventh day, the chosen shamash was so nervous, it couldn't speak at all. The other candles said, "You can do it!" It took a big, big, big breath, stood tall, and lit the seven candles. Proud it had done its job, it melted away in *peace*.

On the eight day, the final candle picked to be the shamash said,

"Friends, how am I going to do this?" And the other candles

said, "This is a big honor, to light the candles on the last day. Be

strong and courageous! You can do it!"

The shamash took a big, big, big, big breath, stood super tall, and with all its heart, with all its soul, and with all its might, lit the eight candles.

Its friends were very proud.

"Thank you for telling me I could do it," the shamash said.

"We believed in you," said the candles.

And proud they had done their jobs,

they all melted away in *delight*.

About the Author

Joelle M. Reizes is a mother of three who writes adult fantasy fiction under the nom de plume JD Blackrose (www.slipperywords. com). Under that name, she wrote *Seder in Space and Other Tales* and contributed a short story to the *Jewish Book of Horror*, as well as writing other Jewish-themed fiction. She spends much of her time herding words into sentences, trying to get them in the correct order. She is Rabbi Joseph Meszler's big sister, although she is a foot shorter.

About the Author

Rabbi Joseph B. Meszler is the spiritual leader of Temple Sinai in Sharon, MA, a noted Jewish educator, and a human rights activist. He is passionate about social justice and interfaith dialogue, fighting hunger and reducing gun violence. Rabbi Meszler has been a Brickner Fellow through the Religious Action Center of Reform Judaism, is a member of the Hevraya of the Institute for Jewish Spirituality, and served as a Global Justice Fellow with American Jewish World Service in 2017–18. He married with two children. He is Joelle M. Reizes' younger brother, but he is a foot taller.

Rabbi Meszler is the author of several books and many articles, including *The Honey Bee and the Apple Tree* (Prospective Press, 2021).

About the Illustrator

Kris Graves has been drawing since they were a tiny sprite. After winning a county-wide art competition in the fourth grade, they set their sights on a life of artistry and cats. *Courageous Candles* is their second illustrated book.

9 781635 160062